George C Bush

Bible Baptism Never Immersion

George C Bush

Bible Baptism Never Immersion

ISBN/EAN: 9783337171681

Printed in Europe, USA, Canada, Australia, Japan

Cover: Foto ©Lupo / pixelio.de

More available books at **www.hansebooks.com**

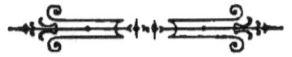

BIBLE BAPTISM NEVER IMMERSION.

BY

REV. GEO. C. BUSH.

———

PHILADELPHIA:

THE JAS. B. RODGERS PRINTING COMPANY,

52 and 54 North Sixth Street.

1888.

CONTENTS.

INTRODUCTION.

THE writer of this Book is a believer in baptism with water. He writes to confirm like believers, and, if possible, to convince others that this is the better way. The Church is to see eye to eye. She is to reach this unity by clearer views. It is hoped this work may contribute something to this glorious result. The writer would neither injure nor disband the beloved Christians calling themselves the Baptist Church. He has preached for and labored with them. He seeks only to have them come into better views and more charitable practices, hastening that day when the people of God shall be one in communion as they are all one in spirit.

GEO. C. BUSH.

West Chester, Pa., June 16, 1888.

1*

BAPTISM.

CHAPTER I.

THE ONE BAPTISM.

WHILE baptism with water was practiced by the Apostles, yet baptism by
the Spirit is oftener mentioned. Dr. Pep-
per, a Baptist writer, says truly, Gospel and
Ordinances are the same thing in *two forms.*
If all our Baptist friends had held this
truth, Prof. Dagg would not write, "Now
there is a baptism of the Spirit; if water
baptism is a perpetual ordinance, then there
are two baptisms instead of one." Nor
would Dr. Carson so mistake as to write, "If
there is such a thing as infant baptism, there
must be two baptisms." Infant and adult

baptisms are no more two than American and English are two. Nor should another author, R. Ingham, conclude, " If this one baptism was by the Spirit, then Paul was guilty of an omission, nay, of a misstatement." The Fathers taught truly (as Jerome) " since all have been baptized into one body, they have received the same Spirit." And Ignatius writes, " There is one baptism, that which is given into the death of our Lord."

The one baptism is the blessed work of the Holy Spirit baptizing us into Christ and so into His body the Church. He who wrote to the Ephesians, there is one baptism, wrote the same truth more fully to the Corinthians. By one Spirit are we all baptized into one body, and have all been made to drink into one Spirit. 1 Cor. 12 : 13. In Gal. 3 : 27, he writes that this baptism is into Christ. Rom. 6 : 3 explains it farther, As many of us as have been baptized into Christ, have been baptized into His death. This baptism gives us all the benefits of

Christ's death. It is as if we died, were buried, and rose again, with sins all forgiven and forsaken, to walk in newness of life.

This one baptism is effected by the Holy Ghost. The Greeks said that wine-drinking baptized, taking an opiate baptized; so the Apostle follows Greek usage, saying in connection with baptism, we drink into one spirit. Many copies leave out the preposition into. Thus it is exact Greek usage to say the baptism was by drinking the one Spirit.

CHAPTER II.

BAPTISM BY THE SPIRIT—ITS MODE. WHAT ARE THE MODAL ACTS OF THIS BAPTISM?

OUR Baptist friends warn us off from such an examination, saying (Dr. Carson) "it is a figurative expression. Believers are said to be immersed into the Spirit, not because there is anything like immersion in the manner of the reception of the Spirit,"—"there can be no likeness to it in the literal baptism."

What is the meaning of such phrases?

1. The one great baptism which Jesus effects by His Spirit is only figurative, not real, like man's baptism.

2. This figurative baptism is a figure that can have no correspondence to that which is figured—a figure which has no likeness to the

10

reality. What man, in his reason, ever used such a figure? How wrong to impute such a violation of propriety to the Holy Spirit!

3. His writing "immersed into the Spirit" contradicts Scripture. We are baptized into Christ, not into the Spirit. The Spirit is the baptizing agent, not the receiving element. Dr. C. errs here as he does about Pentecost baptism, calling it immersion into emblems of the Spirit. What idea has an immersionist of immersion into emblems! This is as ridiculous as the Doctor's idea of Israel's baptism in the sea, calling it a "dry dip." Pentecost baptism was not into emblems of the Spirit, but baptism by the Spirit.

4. But the gravest error of such writing is calling the baptism of the Spirit figurative. If there is anything most positively real, real in the experience of Christians and essential in the teachings of our Lord, it is this very baptism of the Spirit. The two great transactions revealed in Scripture are 1st, the death of Christ to save sinners, and 2d, the application of that death in the

blood of sprinkling by the Holy Spirit. Let no man depreciate the chiefest of God's doings.

But despite the warning not to investigate, we examine the modal acts ascribed to the Spirit. As it is the one baptism of which water baptism is the symbol, its modal acts may be our guide.

John said, I baptize with water, Jesus shall baptize you with the Holy Ghost. Here the contrast is not in the mode, but in the instrument. Both John and Jesus *baptized*, one with water, the other with the Holy Ghost. Our Lord said, Acts 11 : 16, John baptized with water, but ye shall be baptized with the Holy Ghost. Peter says, Acts 11 : 15, the Holy Ghost fell on Cornelius and friends as on us at the beginning. Causing the Holy Spirit to fall on Cornelius was the same in *mode* as that of Pentecost. This baptism was effected by the Spirit's being *poured out*. Acts 2: 17. This was prophesied by Joel. Peter says that prophecy of pouring out the Spirit was that day

fulfilled. This baptism was by *pouring out,*
Acts 10: 45, or falling upon, Acts 10: 44. So
the Samaritans, Acts 8: 16, 17, received
the Holy Spirit by his falling upon them.
Ez. 11: 5, says, The Spirit fell upon me.
Prophets and Christians received the Spirit
by his falling upon—being poured upon
them. And this is called a baptism by
John and Peter and by our Lord. Are
they competent witnesses? "No dipping,
no baptism," is disclaimed by this testimony.

In John 16: 7, our Lord said, I will
send the Comforter. Acts 2: 33, records
"having received of the Father the promise
of the Holy Ghost, he hath *shed forth* this
which ye now see and hear. Again the baptism of the Spirit is called an anointing.
Acts 10 : 38. God anointed Jesus with the
Holy Ghost. Pouring oil upon kings
anointed them for their office. *Pouring* the
Spirit upon Jesus was his anointing. So he
is called The Anointed ; in Greek, Christos ;
in Hebrew, Messiah. Anointing is then the

2

equivalent of the Spirit's coming upon—baptizing him.

Another word often describes this modal act. Matt. 3: 16. Jesus saw the Spirit *descending* like a dove. John 1 : 33. John the Baptist saw the Spirit *descending* from heaven. Here the descent of the Spirit was Christ's baptism by the Spirit, and the proof that he should baptize with the Holy Ghost. Here the modal act was the *descent* of the Spirit. So common is this idea of Spiritual baptism, that a Baptist Conference in England lately sent salutations to one here, " praying the descent of the baptism of the Spirit upon them." Christians think alike, pray alike, and send salutations correctly about the " one baptism," of which water baptism is only the profession. Acts 10: 47, teaches that Peter was moved to apply water baptism by seeing the baptism of the Spirit fall on (v. 44), poured out (v. 45). Did he reason thus, because I have seen Jesus pour out His Spirit, therefore, I will immerse them.? How absurd to represent that outpouring of the Spirit by any ceremony with water if the water was not poured also! An immersion could have no correspondence. It would be a contradiction.

It confirms this view to consider that purifying in the Old Testament is effected in the same way. Is. 52 : 15, He shall sprinkle many nations. Ez. 36 : 25, I will sprinkle clean water upon you. Hos. 14: 5, I will be as the dew. Ps. 72 : 6, He shall come down like rain.

Now the dear friends, whom we would fain win to see eye to eye with us, believe these texts describe the modal acts of the Spirit. Let baptize with water, have the same modal acts, and the barrier between churches is cast down. If baptism with water is made like that of the Spirit, then the water should be poured out, caused to fall on, to sprinkle, to descend as dew, as rain, as pure water.

This view is confirmed by considering that the record always is baptism *with*, not *in,* water. The water is always like the Spirit—the instrument. Baptisms may be into Paul, into Moses, into Christ's death. But there is no record of a baptism *into* water. It is vain to say baptize has the power to carry one under water, when the constant usage of Scripture makes the baptizing instrument *descend.* The Greeks also used baptize where there was no immersion in water. They said one was baptized with wine and taxes and tears and questions and griefs and vice. They understand baptize to indicate a change, not in one mode, but in any mode. Chrysostom, the eloquent Greek preacher, said John was baptized by putting his hand in baptism on the head of our Lord. The Fathers said that all waters were baptized by the baptism of Jesus. They did not mean immersed, but consecrated. Do men now know Greek better than the Greeks? Would Scripture describe the one baptism of the Spirit as a descent, a falling upon, a pouring out, if a valid baptism was the exact reverse?

But this position is strengthened by the representations of our Lord's baptism, in the most ancient churches. In them all, John stands pouring water upon Jesus. Some of these pictures are believed to have been made in the fourth and fifth centuries. Constantine and the Empress are represented as sitting in a bath, while Eusebius pours the water of baptism. As the Corinthians exaggerated the supper, so Constantine added to the rite by getting into a bath. But what was the essence of his baptism? Surely it was the application of water and pronouncing the words of consecration—I baptize thee.

This position is confirmed also by the "Teaching of the Twelve Apostles," that wonderful book compiled, it is supposed, about A.D. 150. Chapter vii. teaches : " Now concerning baptism, so baptize, speaking first all these things, baptize into the name of the Father and Son and Holy Spirit, with living water. If thou hast not living water, baptize with reference to other water;

2*

and if thou art not able with cold, with warm. If thou hast not both, then pour upon the head water into the name of the Father and Son and Holy Spirit. And before the baptism, let the baptizer and the baptized and some others, if they can, fast: But command the baptized to fast one or two days before." Living water, John 4: 10, means water not *stagnant*, a type of grace.

Here the instrument, water, is given in the very form used in the New Testament. It is *en hudati*, with water, not *in*, nor *into* water. As our Lord baptized with the Spirit, so John and the twelve and the early Church baptized *with* water. If the Spirit was poured, or sprinkled, or shed forth, or descended, then reason would teach that the other instrument, water, be applied in like manner. If not, then baptize has one meaning in connection with the Spirit and an entirely opposite meaning connected with water. If not, then things equal to the same things are not equal to one another. If not, then baptize with the Spirit covers one set of actions, as giving, pouring, sprinkling; but with water, an incongruous set of actions, as form a procession, march to some water, descend into it, and immerse the unimmersed part into the water. Surely there is nothing in such an operation like pouring out, shedding forth the Holy Spirit. But things equal to the same thing must be equal to one another. Dr. Carson and friends have said a thousand times, baptizo always means the same thing. Some say dip; others say immerse, and others plunge. While they jostle each other and are all equally positive, yet they all agree that baptizo ought to have one consistent meaning. Now, the constant use of it, in describing the work of the Spirit, forbids any such modal acts as marching to the water, dipping in water. The Bible teaches modal acts utterly opposite. The believer does not go to the Spirit, does not descend into the Spirit, is not immersed in the Spirit. But the Spirit descends, comes, falls upon, is poured out. Surely baptizo cannot cover one set of actions in spiritual baptism and a perfectly opposite and contradictory set of actions when water is the instrument. We hold our Baptist brethren to their proclamation: "Baptizo has one meaning in all literature—in all administrations." And let them say Amen, when we say that in the "one baptism," baptizo means the application of the Spirit to the candidate, never the opposite; and in the profession of spiritual baptism, the modal acts must correspond—the water must be applied.

INFERENCES:—

1. The great body of Christians have administered baptism scripturally, when causing water to descend.

2. "The definite act theory—putting one under water"—is at variance with all Scripture, which uses many words to execute baptism.

3. The definition of baptism in the Baptist Confession, "dipping the whole body under water," is wrong. There is no dipping under

the Spirit. There should be none under water.

4. Messrs. Booth and Wayland saying baptism is "the immersion," are in conflict with the meaning of baptizo in Scripture.

5. Dr. Conant errs saying "baptizo means simply put into or under water." Baptisms by the Spirit are without water. The Greeks used the word to denote the influence of an opiate and wine and taxes and debts and doubts and griefs. What folly to say it means simply to put under water. The Bible has not a record of baptism under water.

CHAPTER III.

BAPTIZO—ITS MEANING.

THIS word occurs about eighty times in the New Testament. It describes baptisms effected by the Spirit—by John—by the Apostles, by Ananias and by Paul.

Seeing the Spirit poured out upon Cornelius and friends made Peter say, " Who can forbid water that these should not be baptized who have received the Holy Ghost as well as we?" The baptism of the Spirit, then, was the model and the reason. The baptism of Saul, when blind and fasting for three days, was effected by Ananias coming and saying, "Why tarriest thou; arise and be baptized : And, *rising up*, he was baptized." Acts 9 : 18. This is the literal translation, indicating the standing posture in Saul's baptism.

22

The baptism of the eunuch was at some water in the desert-way to Gaza: Acts 8. But coming to some, he said, " See, water; what doth hinder me to be baptized?" Then both Philip and the eunuch descended to it, and Philip baptized him. Take baptism to be a profession of the work of the Spirit, then the water was applied to the eunuch, not the reverse. He had been reading in the prophecy of Isaiah, among other things, that Jesus should sprinkle many nations; sprinkling for purification he had seen at Jerusalem. Did he think of Jesus as our High Priest, and would he not wish to profess the work of our Lord by being sprinkled? Had he received the truth that Christ washes us with His own blood : Rev. 1: 5; and would he think of any other way of professing that " blood of sprinkling " than the way named by Isaiah and practiced at Jerusalem?

Moreover, consider the inconvenience of an immersion for one who was at once to ascend his chariot to ride. And no traveler has ever found in that way water enough for an immersion. There are springs, but no lake or river. The very exclamation, see water, indicates a limited quantity. This, put with the fact that he had seen the type of our high priest sprinkle for purification and the fact that the eunuch was reading the prophecy which said Jesus should sprinkle, makes it very evident that the eunuch would expect to be baptized as he saw purification effected at Jerusalem.

The baptism of three thousand at Pentecost, how was it? The Apostles saw the multitudes baptized by the Spirit falling on them. Could they think of professing that work without causing water to descend? If Jesus baptized by pouring out the Spirit, the apostles should baptize by pouring the water.

Besides, consider the improbability of the hated disciples being allowed to use the city reservoirs! Besides the hatred of the new sect, how unlikely that a people so fastidious about purifications should allow three thousand to be plunged into their fountains?

If baptism can be executed sometimes by immersion, yet there were no conditions for such a baptism in that mountain city under the control of bitter enemies. But baptism is executed in pouring out the Spirit and sending tongues of fire upon the heads of the disciples. So said John and Jesus. How improbable that the twelve would have this work professed by an immersion which had nothing in common with what was promised and with what they had seen!

When Jesus said, ye shall be baptized with the Holy Ghost, he meant that very work of Pentecost. Is baptism then essentially the act of putting under water? Joel and John and Jesus and Peter testify to a baptism where the Spirit fell and where tongues of fire sat. Are they not sufficient witnesses?

1 Cor. 10 : 2 teaches that all Israel was baptized into Moses, with the cloud and with the sea. The same preposition en used here occurs in the promise, he shall baptize you, en, with the Holy Ghost. The cloud and the sea were the instruments, not the receiving

3

element. The cloud stood behind and the waters of the sea were walls on each side. Here was a baptism without water—Baptist authority says "a dry dip." But there was no dip—but a march—the people, it is thrice recorded, passed through on dry ground. Ex. 14: 22, 29, and 15: 19. Polybius says Alexander's army was baptized all day marching through a lake—Israel was baptized marching all night in a waterless sea. Both Alexander's army and Israel would have perished in an immersion. The miracle of the cloud and the sea moved Israel to believe the Lord and His servant Moses. Ex. 13. Here was baptism of parents and children that preceded faith and induced faith. And this baptism the Apostle of the Gentiles commends. Did Paul then know that baptism meant the definite act of putting a believer into water? He records a baptism without water that made the people believe.

1 John 5: 8 says the Spirit and the water and the blood bear witness, and these three agree in one. The Spirit is shed forth—

poured out—the blood is sprinkled. Now how can water in an immersion agree with the Spirit or the blood? Immersion makes the water contradict the mode of applying both. Does Jesus shed His blood and pour out His Spirit? To agree with that work, then, water should be applied also. The Greek Bible used by the Apostles says Nebuchadnezzar was baptized with the dew. Origen, one of the most learned of the Fathers, says that Elijah's altar was baptized. Neither Nebuchadnezzar nor the altar were dipped. Did the seventy who translated the Hebrew into Greek understand Greek? Was Origen behind the times to think and call Elijah's altar baptized? How absurd to say " no immersion, no baptism." The Greek Bible, the Greek Fathers and the Greek Classics, with the cloud and the sea, thunder their negative to the monstrous statement.

Luke 11: 38, Jesus was invited to dine with a Pharisee who marvelled that before eating he did not baptize (E baptiza). Mark 7 : 2, has the same charge against the disciples for eating with hands unwashed. Tradition required that one should cleanse himself oft or diligently or up to the elbows. (See margin, verse 3.) Yea, they eat not when they come from the market except they baptize themselves (baptizontai). The Syriac Bible, for hundreds of years, used rantizontai—sprinkled themselves. That early church interchanged these words. And Mark 7 : 4. records further, that the Pharisees held to baptism (baptismous) of cups and pots and brazen vessels and tables. Tradition required the Jews to purify themselves and dishes before eating. Mark uses baptizo and baptismos to denote that purification. John 13 uses niphso to describe the washing of the disciples' feet, to denote that they were clean. John 13 : 10. That washing was not an immersion. Tables were not immersed for purification. But Mark says their purification was a baptism.

Heb. 9 : 10, informs us that in the Jewish service there were divers baptisms. They could not be divers (Greek diaphorois, diverse, different) if they were a simple immersion. Baptisms were administered in different ways in the Jewish ceremonies. There is not an immersion among them, and yet they are baptisms (baptismos). Heb. 9 specifies baptism by sprinkling blood and water and ashes—affirming that they purified the flesh as Christ's blood purges the conscience. Num. 19 : 16–20, directs how to purify one defiled from the dead. Take running water and put it to the ashes of the burnt heifer and sprinkle the impure for his cleansing. Josephus, 4 : 4, 6, calls this ceremony baptizing from the dead. Did Josephus understand the Jewish religion? Is putting running water to the ashes of an heifer and sprinkling the unclean an immersion? Josephus says it was a baptism. Where washing the body was part of the ceremony of purification, still the sprinkling was the most essential thing. See Num. 19. And their washings for forty years in the desert were not and could not be immersions. In the whole history of the human family washing is usually without immersion.

The New Testament uses about eighty verbs ending in zo. Like baptizo, they have many meanings. Katharizo is translated to purge, to cleanse, to purify; euaggelizo, by preach and five other words; emphanizo, by show and nineteen other words; chorizo, by put and thirteen other words. Why must baptizo be limited? Dr. Conant, it is said, uses about forty words to translate the classic baptizo. How wrong, then, to affirm that this word in baptism must mean only an immersion! Baptizing from the dead did not mean an immersion; baptizing tables did not mean an immersion; baptizing Elijah's altar was not an immersion. Divers baptisms were not all immersions. If Moses baptized almost all things by sprinkling blood and ashes and water, what folly to affect a wisdom superior to Moses, saying, " No immersion no baptism"! Bathing in the crowded camps and in the waterless desert could not have been an immersion.

Seirax 31: 30. Being baptized from the dead and again touching it, what profit is the (loutron) washing? Here washing equals baptizing. The most important part of this purification we have seen was sprinkling. Seirax calls it a baptism. Rev. 1 : 5, Christ hath washed us from our sins *with* (en, same form John used) his blood. Eph. 5: 26, Christ cleanses the Church with the washing of water by the word. This (loutron) washing-baptism is by the word. There is no immersion in the word.

But the appeal is carried from the court of Scripture to the usage of the Greeks. To that court we will go. Look at the definition of baptizo in twenty-two lexicons. One of the most common is merge. This is its meaning when followed by the preposition *into.* This is the force of the word when the baptism is into Christ, into Moses, into Paul, into the Church. It is not a plunge into Christ, not an immersion in His blood, not a dip into the Church. If we were merged in water as we are in Christ, we should be devoted to and permanently fixed in the water. One stream is merged in another when it unites and flows in the same channel. There is no merging of believers with the Jordan. One title is merged in another when it is combined in the one owner. But immersion has nothing like such mergings of streams and titles. One stream is not dipped in another; it is united and merged in the other.

Baptizo is also translated bathe and wash. These verbs are executed by washing the body or the feet or the hands. They were common among the Jews from Sinai to the Jordan. There are no lakes or rivers in the whole route. Such a purity for worship, Heb. x., requires, "Having your bodies washed with pure water." An immersion, with the clothes on, is no more washing the body with pure water than is rolling it in the street. A real washing this text requires. A dipping is not obedience to it.

Baptizo is also translated from the classics by *immerse.* But we see that this meaning agrees neither with Jewish washings, nor traditional purifications, nor with the baptism of the Spirit. While it is one of many definitions of the word, we see it is entirely inadequate to answer for baptizo in its religious uses.

But how unreasonable is it to pitch upon one meaning out of more than a dozen and say, they are not in the church of Christ who will not immerse? Most dictionaries give from six to sixteen definitions of baptizo. Who has the authority to limit us to one meaning? As a mild specimen of this dogmatism, take Prof. Curtis. He gives Passow's definitions "dip repeatedly, dip under, bathe, steep, wet, pour upon ; 2. dip, draw water ; 3. N. T., baptize." He then concludes, " Baptizo means dip, sink, immerse and nothing else, and the command, to be baptized is to be immersed, if it is anything." But why does not Professor Curtis say the command is to sink. Passow says sink. Why not say it is to steep or to wet or to pour upon ? Passow says baptizo means any of these. How arbitrary is it to seize on one and unchurch all who take to wet or to pour upon as a good meaning!

Liddell and Scott define baptizo, " dip in or under water, sink, bathe, soak in wine, fall into debt, puzzle with questions; 2, draw water or wine; 3, baptize." Suppose a sect should take puzzle as the meaning, and insist that asking questions executed baptism. Or suppose a sect took soak in wine, what a nice religion that would make? Or take falling into debt as a baptism, how very pious would many people and churches be found? The truth is, baptizo denotes a change by some controlling influence as wine, an opiate, tears, water, taxes, griefs, etc. To be baptized is to come under the influence of that which baptizes. In ritual purification it is with water to be devoted to God. The quantity has no more influence in effecting a baptism with water than the length of the sentence has in a baptism by question. A tax of fifty dollars may baptize *one* as easily as a tax of a thousand *another* A small seal may authenticate a deed as well as one spread over half a sheet. The water is a sign of spiritual purification, a profession of the work of the Spirit, of cleansing by the blood of sprinkling, a token of the "one baptism."

Robinson's Dictionary defines baptizo, " dip in, sink, immerse, draw water, wash, lave, cleanse, middle and passive, voice wash one's self, *i. e.*, hands or persons, perform ablution. 2. Baptize, administer baptism." Of these various meanings, who would not prefer wash to denote purity? Robinson gives " dip in " as one meaning. When the Baptist Confession was made, they seized upon this meaning. But Booth, a Baptist, writes, "This makes our sentiment and practice ridiculous." Yet the ridiculous dip is the practice under the name of immerse.

Deipnon, supper, in Greek, was the principal meal. Yet the Holy Spirit calls the memorial of our Lord's death a supper. The Corinthians made a feast of it, taking the word in its widest meaning. They were corrected for their literality. But how much like them are those who make the other sacrament an immersion? But if this extreme meaning must be taken, as in the dark ages, let the washing be thorough, as then, men washing nude men, and women their companions, before the minister sprinkled the candidate, as then was done, saying, I baptize thee. With them, as among the Jews, the washing was a preparation for the more essential sprinkling.

The dictionaries, we see, decide that baptizo has many meanings. We trust it is evident enough that we are not bound by any dictionary to execute baptism by any particular word of the sixteen given as English equivalents. Robinson's last definition is baptize. This is the word in the Latin, Italic, French and English Bibles. Why try to put any other in its room? Dr. Carson, the most able Baptist writer, after saying baptizo signifies "dip, never expressing anything but mode," added wisely, "I have all the lexicographers and commentators against me." Dictionaries give from six to sixteen meanings to the word. Baptist authors write out these meanings and then found their creed and practice on one of them ; and then affirm, if any other meaning is allowed, it is such a willful sin that it excludes you from the church of God! The Fathers said there were as many kinds of baptism as of doctrines. The Holy Spirit says there were differing baptisms in Israel's service. But now we must believe that the Holy Spirit erred in saying there were divers baptisms ; dictionaries erred also, for baptizo cannot be performed except in one way.

We have examined baptizo in dictionaries. They do not limit the meaning to immerse. Robinson and others say it means to draw water. May we seize on that definition and make baptism the act of drawing water? How much better his other definition, to cleanse, to wash? Then the application of water harmonizes with the cleansing professed. Our Lord washed the disciples' feet to denote that they were clean. John xiii.

4

This was not an immersion. Pilate washed his hands to denote innocence. This was no immersion. We have Old Testament and New Testament, we have dictionaries, commentators and churches—we have Greeks, Romans and Jews all agreeing that baptism is a ceremonial washing. Why divide the kingdom for another meaning?

TAKE A BIBLE READING.

1 Pet. 1: 2, Elect unto obedience and sprinkling of the blood of Jesus Christ. 1 John 1: 7, The blood of Jesus Christ cleanseth us from all sin. Heb. 9 : 14, How much more shall the blood of Christ purge your conscience from dead works to serve the living God? What does Jesus do? He sprinkles His blood—He washes us from our sins—cleanses from all sin—purges the conscience. What did John the Baptist call this work? Is he good authority? John called it a baptism. What did Jesus call the outpouringof the Spirit upon the one hundred and twenty? Is He a credible witness? He called it a baptism. He used baptizo to

describe that work. Is baptism then a dipping and nothing but dipping? Is the Holy Ghost in fault in calling purification with the Spirit and with blood a baptism? Must we go blindly against all Scripture and all learning to enter the fold of Christ?

Josephus 18 : 5, 2, writes of John's baptism, "The washing with water would be acceptable to God, if they made use of it, not in order to the putting away or the remission of some sins only, but for the purification of the body, supposing still that the soul was thoroughly purified by righteousness." What did water signify in John's baptisms? Josephus says the purification. Josephus, is there any purification by immersion in the laws of Moses? None. Josephus, what was Jewish law for purifying? Bathing the body and sprinkling the water of separation? Num.19. Josephus did not understand John to sing, .

> "Ho, every son and daughter,
> Here's the gospel in the water."

Prof. Strong's able work on Theology is

marred by the assertion of such absurd state-
ments as "Christian baptism is the immersion of a believer in water." "The mode is
immersion only." "Christ's baptism was
consecration to death." Jesus said it was to
fulfill all righteousness. He therein devoted
himself to His life-work, not to death. True
death was the end of that work. But it is
to contradict the record to say His baptism .
was consecration to death.

Prof. Strong affirms that "baptism denot-
ing influence without intus-position (immersion) is a figment of the imagination."

How can a scholar write such a sentence,
when he knows that the Greeks used baptizo
to denote the influence of wine and debts
and taxes and sleep and vice and opiates.
Is it a figment of the imagination that wine
baptizes without an immersion, or that sleep
stupefies, or an opiate affects one without an
immersion in the stupefying drug? When
the Greeks for a thousand years used baptizo
to denote a change produced in the mind by
grief and by fears, and by questions and by

debts and by taxes, what folly is it to affirm that baptizo means an immersion! Prof. Strong relies for proof upon the partial admission of some who are not Baptists. Judge how much such admissions are worth against the texts and dictionaries before quoted. We say *partial* admissions, because many did not intend to give full sanction to immersion, but, like the dictionaries, to say that one meaning of baptizo is to immerse. Prof. Strong quotes Dean Stanley; yet Dean Stanley told the Baptist brethren, in New York, that the Church wisely changed the practice of immersion of the dark ages. Prof. Strong quotes De Stourdza, saying baptizo means to plunge. Then he concludes it means nothing but to *immerse*. To plunge is not to immerse. If he plunged candidates, the society for the prevention of cruelty would soon interfere.

But it seems the great mind of Dr. Strong, like others, can quote meanings of baptizo conflicting with immersion and then complacently assume, against all the Greeks, baptizo means to immerse only. Prof. Strong says

4*

that baptism without intus-position (immersion) is a figment of the imagination. The New Testament speaks of the baptism of tables, of *divers* baptisms, of the baptism of Israel marching on dry ground. Were these baptisms by immersion? Surely no man, unless his eyes were filled with water, could so see it.

The New Testament very often speaks of the work of the Spirit as a baptism. We have seen that the modal acts of this baptism are utterly opposite to immersion. He descends, is poured out, comes as rain and as dew. Nebuchadnezzar was wet with the dew; baptized is the word in the Greek Bible used by our Lord. Prof. Strong translates " baptized *in* water and *in* the Holy Spirit." *En,* in the New Testament, is used over three hundred times before words to denote instrumentality.

Christians are evangelized by the Spirit, not in; sanctified by, not in; filled with, not in, led by, not in, justified by, not in. How it contradicts the usage of Scripture to say, baptized *in*, not *by* the Spirit? Read 1 Cor. 12: 13, with this idea. " For *in* one spirit are we all baptized into one body." Was it *in* or *by* one Spirit, the baptism was effected? What strange changes immersion requires? When the' preposition en is used over three hundred times, translated by, or through, or with; yet immersion must make it violate this usage.

Prof. Strong summons Dr. Coleman as witness that immersion was the practice of the early churches. Hear him, page 367 : "The Church soon lost the spirituality of her religion and the simplicity of her ordinances, in endless strifes about forms and ceremonies. Perhaps the first of all her departures from the institutions of Christ and His apostles was to insist upon immersion as emblematic of the suffusion of the Holy Spirit and the only valid mode of administering the ordinance. Certain it is that this soon became the prevailing mode of baptizing. Other changes soon followed," etc. How many witnesses like this would establish immersion ?

That we are not shut up to translate baptizo by immerse, is manifest also from such
facts as these :

1. Some dictionaries do not give immerse
as its meaning. Could this be its most essential meaning, and lexicographers not
know it ?

2. Comparing the frequency of its occur-
rence, we see that dictionaries give the pref-
erence to other words. Twenty of them give
immerse four times ; baptize, six times ; perform ablutions, eight times ; merge, eight
times ; lave, fourteen times. Immerse cannot be its most essential meaning, else the
dictionaries would give it oftener. A merging is not an immersion, else why do they
give merge ? To perform ablutions, with
Jews and pagans, differed from an immersion. Else why give this meaning eight
times to immerse four ? To lave, the world
over, is oftener performed without than with
a dipping. If baptizo meant essentially immerse, why do dictionaries give so many
other definitions ? See also the varied uses

of baptizo. The Greeks said men were baptized with wine, debts, taxes, questions, opiates, sea, milk, fire, sword, spirit, grief, disease, oil, sins, sleep, vice. What did they mean by such baptisms? Did they mean that men were immersed in wine and swords and oil and opiates? Nay; but they meant to indicate the influence from these agents. So baptism by the Spirit means His influence upon us. So baptism with water means devotion by its ritual use to God. Baptized by wine, taxes and griefs means affected by their influence. Baptized into the death of Christ means coming under the influence of his death, so as to die unto sin and live unto righteousness. Baptized into the name of the Father, Son and Holy Ghost is to be devoted to the triune Jehovah. The water of baptism is, then, a symbol of the work of the Spirit applying the blood that washes us from our sins. All sects agreed in England defining baptism to signify and seal our ingrafting into Christ and our partaking of the benefits of the covenant of grace, and our engagement to be the Lord's. As our Baptist brethren make baptizo their stronghold, we turn on it definitions given by Greek dictionaries. Suidas, of the tenth century, gives pluno, to wash, as the essential meaning.

Gases, a member of the Greek Church, in his large dictionary in two volumes, defines baptizo by three Latin words: 1, Brecho, to wet, to bedew, to moisten; 2, Lavo, to wash, to bathe; 3, Antleo, to draw, to pump water.

How true was the confession of Dr. Carson, "I have all the lexicographers and commentators against me." Yes, the Greeks give no aid to the men that assume immerse as the essential meaning of baptizo. They do not give immergo, immerse, as even one of its meanings! How utterly impossible is it that immerse is its most essential meaning if a quarto Greek lexicon did not record it! How wonderfully wise have men become that can define Greek better than men that spoke Greek—better than men that wrote the dictionary of their native tongue!

CHAPTER IV

BAPTIZO EN—BAPTIZE IN AND WITH.

BAPTIZO en—with places, means baptize in, as Enon, Salim, Bethabara, the Jordan, beyond Jordan, and wilderness. These names of places, except in the river Jordan, forbid the idea of immersion. And when immersion is eliminated from baptism in so many places it is reasonable to understand in the Jordan means also the place, not the manner of baptism. This is confirmed by the Gospels' using two other prepositions as well as en. In Matt. 3 : 13, the record is, "then came Jesus from Galilee" (epi) upon Jordan. Mark 1 : 9 has (eis) at or to Jordan. If we render it *to* Jordan, it will respond then to "came," preceding. If we read it at or in, then it will denote the place. These places, except in the Jordan, exclude immersion. And in some seasons an immersion is impossible in the Jordan. A dear Baptist brother was greatly offended when a traveler told us the Jordan was only about two feet deep when he waded it. Why?

But Baptizo en means "baptize with," when used with the baptizing instrument— as water, Holy Spirit, cloud and sea. 1 Cor. 10: 2, baptized en—with—the cloud and with the sea. It is the same form as in the gospels. The Bible has no instance of *in* water. It is always *with* water. Some texts omit the preposition, using only the instrumental dative (hudati) with water. If immersion in water was the only right baptism, then the Scripture is wrong in using the instrumental dative! At least, we ought to find one record of such a baptism, if such only is valid. Bible baptisms are with the Spirit poured out, or with water to profess it, or with the sea on either hand, or with the cloud in the rear while the feet of Israel marched on dry ground. How perfectly and utterly we reverse the very letter of Scripture if we affirm that these baptisms were "immersions in or under water."

CHAPTER V.

BAPTIZO EIS—BAPTIZE INTO.

THESE words mark the result of baptism. Baptized into Christ's death means that we share the benefits of that death. Baptized into Christ's body means that we are made members of His body. Gal. 3 : 27, the baptized into Christ have put on Christ. They are in Him, having His righteousness. Baptized into forgiveness means the state of forgiveness. Baptized into the remission of sins and into repentance and into Paul and into Moses are expressions of the *state* of the baptized towards Moses and Paul and repentance.

The Bible has no record of baptized *into water*. Eis hudor is not found in the Bible. But our immersion brethren in thought and intention and in practice always insert *into water*. Is it not an unwarrantable license to add *into water* when Scripture never uses the words? If immersion into water was the *sine qua non* of baptism, surely we should have had one example. Our brethren disagree about the meaning of the prepositions used with baptizo as well as about the verb itself. Some says eis means in ; some, into ; others, unto ; others, in reference to. While they contend with each other for diverse meanings for the verb and for the prepositions, yet they agree that one must be covered to the last hair with water in order to a valid baptism. And all this without an instance of it in the diverse baptisms of Scripture. Baptism into Christ's death, that great work of the Holy Ghost, is belittled to make it a profession of his death and absurdly the candidate is assured that his submission represents Christ on the cross!

CHAPTER VI.

BAPTISMOS.

THIS word is used four times. In Mark 7: it means the ceremonial purification of pots, cups and tables. In Heb. 6: 2, it is used with doctrine, as if doctrine qualified baptisms, just as repentance did in John's ministry. The doctrines mentioned just before were repentance and faith. Heb. 9: 10 means ritual purifications in Jewish service. Among these ablutions it was required that one bathe his body, wash his garments and be sprinkled with the water of separation. Nu. 19. But there is no immersion in Judaism. Baptismos gives no support to the theory,—no dipping, no baptism.

CHAPTER VII

BAPTISMA.

THIS word is used twenty-two times. It describes the ministry of John, as when the Pharisees came to John's baptism. They came to more than a dipping. It also describes the suffering of our Lord. His agony in Gethsemane—His death on Calvary were infinitely more than an immersion in water. Baptisma as John's ministry and baptisma as Christ's sufferings were very different things. Is baptisma then a covering with water? The Fathers used this word to describe martyrdom. They often coveted this baptism. Did they mean an immersion that should strangle them? Yet no idea was more common with these Greek Fathers than that their blood in martyrdom baptized them. A baptisma of blood was where blood was shed in any way. Baptisma into the death of Christ, Rom. 6 : 4, was not a baptism when Christ died, but a union with Him in the merits of His death now effected by the Holy Spirit. There is no record of baptisma *in* or *into* water. And the operation of the Spirit baptizing us into Christ has in it nothing like an immersion. There is no correspondence in time, state or manner between the Spirit's work and a dipping. Every Greek noun, preposition and verb refuses to connect baptism with immersion. They all utterly repudiate any communion with the dipping theory.

CHAPTER VIII.

IMMERSION. WHY INTRODUCED?

PURIFICATION under the Old Testament was usually effected by sprinkling ashes, water or blood. Priests were purified by washing hands and feet at the door of the tabernacle. Jesus said of His washing Peter's feet, If I wash thee not thou hast no part with me. Peter then cried out, Not my feet only, but my hands and my head. He reasoned, If some washing is good, then let me have more. Baptists are not followers of John, but of Peter. They practice baptism into water—John practiced baptism with water. They use bapto eis, he used baptizo en. The Fathers' writings show that even when they used immersion, in some cases they baptized the sick upon their

55

beds. They held that all waters baptized. They fell into Peter's error in practice, yet they never taught that the mode of applying the water was essential. Some added exorcism and anointing, and trine immersion, one for each person of the Trinity. What did they mean by baptize? They meant bringing a person into a holy state by the water and Spirit coacting upon the person. They thought washing the body would absorb more virtue. Therefore, they made not an immersion only, but a real washing.

For many years the Baptists did not immerse. They assert that the English Baptists made the change in 1641. Till then this sect practiced baptism as did other churches. They seem to have introduced immersion one hundred years after their origin in Germany, to separate their church from others with a wider mark of distinction. Yet the most of them in England to this day do not make so much of immersion, do not unchurch all who prefer another of sixteen definitions of baptize rather than immerse. But in this country it is dip, or you cannot be a member of the church of God. Baptized into Moses meant a new disposition in Israel to receive and obey Moses. It was not true that all were immersed in Moses. Nor were the Corinthians immersed or buried or plunged into Paul. Baptized into Christ's body means our union with, our articulation into His church. The virtue of such baptisms is not in the size of Paul or Moses or the church ; but in the new disposition—the new creation by the Spirit. Applying the Baptist immersion, what a perversion of truth to say, All Israel was plunged, dipped, immersed into Moses ! All Christians are by the Spirit baptized into Christ so as to be one in Him. What a caricature of the truth is it to say they are dipped into Christ.

CHAPTER IX.

OUR brethren, of course, have some texts which they use to justify their theory. One is that John baptized in Jordan. Why this record, say they, if it was not an immersion? The answer has been given before. In Jordan designates the place. No Baptist reasons that John immersed in sand from the record that John baptized in the wilderness, nor that he dipped converts in the dust because it is written, John baptized in Bethabara. John baptized in the Jordan, in the river Jordan, not *in* water but *with* water. Brother Curtis has found in Mark 1: 9, baptized and eis (into, or to, or at) in the same verse. But the eis is not connected with water. He has translated eis on the

58

preceding page *at.* But on this page he seizes upon *into* as the meaning. We are sorry to take away his comfort. But if eis means *at* on one page, why may it not on the other ? Brother Curtis not only contradicts himself, but makes Matt. 3 : 13 using epi at, or upon, conflict with Mark. When Matthew says Jesus came from Galilee upon the Jordan, he means the same as Mark saying he came from Galilee and was baptized by John, eis Jordan. Moreover, Prof. Curtis' construction conflicts with all the many representations in ancient churches of our Lord's baptism. He stood at or in Jordan while John poured the baptizing water.

2. A second Baptist reason for immersion is Col. 2 : 12, buried with him in Baptism. It reconciles many to the sad experience of immersion that they not only imitate Christ's baptism, but that they are buried *with Him,* so come nearer to Him in baptism. But Christ is in heaven, not in mill-ponds. He was buried over eighteen hundred years ago

—we cannot be buried bodily with him; moreover, his burial was in a room hewn out of a rock into which Joseph carried his body and rolled a great stone against the door. There is nothing in immersion *like* the burial of Jesus. Moreover, a brief statement is always to be interpreted by one more full. Rom. 6 : 3 tells us we are baptized into Christ's death; verse 4, buried with him by baptism into death; verse 5, planted with him; verse 6, our old man crucified with him; verse 8, died with Christ. Can any of these things be affirmed of water baptism? Neither does Col. 2 : 12 teach anything about water baptism. The Apostle says we are complete in Christ, circumcised in His circumcision, buried with Him in " *the* baptism," raised up in Him, quickened with Him, all trespasses forgiven. Are these attributes of water baptism, even if in an ocean? Nay, but they are attributes of " the " one baptism. " *The* " is in the Greek. If it had been translated it might have saved many from error. Col. 2 teaches us we have all in Christ by faith, which is the operation of God. How absurd, then, is it to say we are buried by dipping and are raised up by faith! But few would ever get out of an immersion if this was the way of escape. Buried with Christ in " *the* baptism " has no more water in it than had baptizing the one hundred and twenty with tongues of fire. *The* baptism that buries us with Christ is the same that crucifies us and raises us up and makes us complete in Him. Water has nothing to do with this baptism but to profess it.

As great dependence is placed on Rom. 6 : 4, we examine the text more carefully. We are buried with Him by baptism into death. What death? Ans., v. 3, Christ's death.

What buries us? Ans. Our baptism—by baptism. When did Christ die? Ans. Over eighteen hundred years ago. Can we be buried bodily with Him in time? Certainly not. Can we be placed bodily in Joseph's tomb? Certainly not. How then are we buried with Him? In the sense that

6

He died and was buried and rose for us. What baptizes us into his death? The Holy Spirit's work. Who administers this baptism? Our ascended Saviour. How does He baptize? By sending, pouring out the Spirit. What does the Spirit do for us? He baptizes, merges into Christ. What is the benefit of this baptism? It makes us complete in Christ? Can water baptism effect such a result? Never. What relation has water baptism to this spiritual work? It can only symbolize and profess it. Can we be buried in water with Christ? Nay, He is in heaven. Can we die on the cross with Jesus? There was none with Him. Can we rise bodily out of water with Him? This is impossible. What is meant by dying with Him, being dead with Him, crucified with Him, complete in Him, buried with Him? It means our perfect union with Him in His sufferings for us, so they were as good to us as our dying under the penalty and rising to a new life. What buries us with Christ? The baptism by the Holy Spirit. Ought water baptism to represent Christ's burial? Nay. Of all things His burial by Joseph has no special significance except to assure us of the reality of His death. Ought baptism to *represent* His death? Nay. The supper is to show forth His death.

3. Another Baptist reason for immersion is 1 Pet. 3: 21. The like figure whereunto even baptism doth now save us. Noah is figured to have been immersed in the flood and drawn out, so Christians now immersed in water are drawn out saved. But Peter says our baptism is not a washing away of the filth of the flesh, but it is the state of the conscience through the resurrection of Jesus Christ. Peter connects this saving work with the finished redemption of our Lord. Moreover, Noah was not immersed. The antediluvians only were immersed, and our brethren themselves own that the baptism of the Spirit alone can save. Peter, then, like Paul, was not speaking of a water baptism that cannot save, but of the baptism of the Spirit.

4. A fourth Baptist reason is found in 1 Cor. 10 : 2. All Israel was baptized into Moses with the cloud and with the sea. The cloud stood between them and the Egyptians, yet baptized them. The sea, in walls miles apart, enclosed them, yet baptized them, so cloud and sea made them believe the Lord and his servant Moses. Ex. 14 : 31. Dr. Conant happily defines this as a baptism bringing into a new state of life and experience. This was the baptism of Israel going through the sea on dry ground. The Egyptians were immersed, not baptized. Israel was not immersed, but baptized with the cloud and sea. Apply Dr. Conant's idea of Israel's baptism to Rom. 6 : 4. It brings into a new state of life. It unites us with Christ.

5. A fifth Baptist reason for immersion is the baptism of the Eunuch. He had been to Jerusalem to worship; he was reading Isaiah's prophecy of Christ. Philip asked him if he understood it. Being invited, he ascended the chariot and explained Isaiah. The Eunuch had seen the priests purify the people by

sprinkling, had read the prophecy that said Christ should sprinkle many nations ; discovering water, he said, See, water; what doth hinder me from being baptized ? Upon his confessing Christ, " they both descended to the water both Philip and the Eunuch, and he baptized him." These words marked are a literal rendering of the Greek. There is no immersion recorded ; there was no preparation of garments for it; there has never been found in that desert water enough for an immersion. How unlikely there was any ? He had seen priests sprinkle ashes, blood, incense and water ; he was reading the prophecy of Christ sprinkling many nations. How naturally, then, he would expect to profess purification in the way he had seen and read of its being done.

6. A sixth reason given for immersion is John 3 : 23. *Much water.* Why much water if it were not for immersion ? The answer is found in the preceding verse recording that Jesus and the crowds attending his ministry were also in the same region. He was now

making more disciples than John, John (4 :
1.) Much water would be needed for the two
great congregations. Enon in Hebrew means
fountains. It is the plural of en—fountain.
Jesus and John could assemble multitudes in
that part of Judea, because there was much
water in these fountains. The learned Am-
brose says there were twelve fountains and
seventy palm-trees. At Elim, Israel came
to twelve fountains. Ex. 15 : 27. Our immersion brethren suppose that these fountains
may have poured their water into reservoirs
sufficient for immersion. John 3 : 23 can
serve immersion, then, only by improbable
guess-work. 1, that Baptizo means here not
any of its many meanings except immerse ;
2, that these fountains drained into a reser-
voir ; and 3, that the mention of these many
springs was for immersion and not for the
drinking and cooking purposes of the great
multitude.

7. A seventh reason given for immersion
is John 3 : 5—*born of water.* The other
part of the verse is born of the Spirit. We

have seen that the Spirit works by coming upon, descending, pouring upon. If this is giving a new creation—a birth into the kingdom—then birth by water should be professed by pouring out, causing to descend. Nicodemus was an inquiring Jew. He found that outward ordinances had not satisfied; he came to ask what farther was necessary. Jesus guides him at once to a purification by the Spirit. It was not yet time to say, all Mosaic observances are ended. But it was time to say that a man must have more than water purification; he must have with it a spiritual purification—so be born of water not only, but of the Spirit. There was no immersion for purification as there is no immersion into the Spirit.

CHAPTER X.

POSTURE IN BAPTISM.

ALL ancient pictures known represent Jesus as *standing* when baptized by John. When he received the baptism of the Spirit he was *going up from* Jordan. The Spirit came on Him while He was *walking*. Classic Greeks speak of armies baptized all day while *marching*. The Spirit baptized the one hundred and twenty at Pentecost when they were *sitting ;* Saul was baptized *standing*.

Now shall we seize on one position, and say baptism must be administered to one standing ? That would make us like some seizing upon one meaning of baptize. What folly to legislate that in baptism the baptized must stand ! Did not Saul stand ? Does not

Luke use the word seventy-nine times, so we can be sure of our posture? Very true—true, this word forbids an immersion. But yet there was a baptism of the Spirit filling the disciples, and with tongues of fire resting upon them where they were *sitting.* Even when the error had crept in that water and Spirit must co-work, yet they baptized the sick upon their couches. But the theory " no dipping no baptism " was not true in any of these baptisms. There is no record of a baptism in lying down. Sitting, standing or walking are Bible postures.

CHAPTER XI.

THE BAPTISM OF CHILDREN.

OUR Baptist brethren deny that children have any such right to ordinances in the New as they had in the Old Testament—that the door of the gospel church breaks all family relations—that we enter the Church without wife or child. And all because it is written " he that believeth and is baptized." They insist that faith in the candidate must precede baptism, because in this one verse faith is mentioned first.

But take the great Commission, Matt. 28, translate it literally. Going disciple all nations, baptizing them into the name of the Father and of the Son and of the Holy Ghost, teaching them to observe. Here baptizing is put before teaching. Must we bap-

tize before we teach ? 1 Cor. 6 : 11, Ye are
washed, ye are sanctified, ye are justified. If
the order of words is an authority, first baptism, then sanctification, then justification.
Is this the divinely appointed order? Here
and in the great Commission our brethren
agree with us that the order is not authori-
tative. Why then rule the children out of
the kingdom by a catch at words? Better
take the order baptize, teach, as in Mat. 28,
or wash, sanctify, in Paul's epistle to Corinth.
Here are two texts putting baptize and wash
before teach. Then the order of words is
two to one in the children's favor.

Our brethren assume that the New Testament made such a change in the administration of God's grace, that the church is a new
institution and the conditions of membership
are changed. But the New Testament and
Old alike teach that the virtue of an ordinance is the state of the heart.—Circumcision denoted the heart's devotion. Why cannot the same principle be applied to the baptism of children? While God commanded

the heart to be circumcised, yet he required circumcision of the flesh on the eighth day. When the Old Testament calls Israel my people, a hundred times—and my chosen— my beloved and saints—how wrong to deny that Israel was a church !

Besides, the New Testament addresses commands to parents and children as equally in the church.   Eph. 6 : 4, Bring up your children *en*, not *eis*, in, not into the nurture and admonition of the Lord.   Lu. 18 : 16, Of such is the kingdom of heaven, *i. e.*, the kingdom belongs to them.   Yet must they be excluded from the very badge of membership? Yea, denied any membership? The effort is made to neutralize this text by saying the kingdom belongs to the childlike.   See the wrong of this interpretation.   *Brephos* is the word that described the infant Saviour in the manger.   The plural is *brepha*.   When parents brought such to Jesus (*brepha* is the word) and the twelve resisted them, Jesus said, suffer the little children to come unto me and forbid them not.   The Apostles thought baby-blessing wrong. But the Master corrected their carnal reasoning. He imparts spiritual blessings to babes, and He says the kingdom of heaven belongs to them. Sad if it is now unlawful to bring them to Jesus. Jesus baptized babes with His Spirit. Is it wrong to profess that spiritual work?

Again consider children were in the covenant of works and fell in Adam. Was the covenant to work only for their condemnation? Is not grace to abound to them even as the evil of the fall has afflicted them? Has the covenant principle no application to them but for ruin? If death reigned by the sin of one, shall not grace reign through our Lord Jesus Christ? Is not this the doctrine of the Holy Spirit in Rom. 5? Is it eternal law that the iniquity of fathers can be visited on children and yet there is no counter-principle of visiting the good of parents?

Also consider that God has always included children in covenant-dealing. As with Adam so with Noah, Abraham and David. When

7

He covenanted with Israel it was with the men not only, but with their wives and little ones. Have the principles of God's government so changed that He cannot embrace children in covenant privileges? The children have rights in all other governments. Have they been ruled out of the best government? What Stephen called the church in the wilderness had blessings for them in the two sacraments, Circumcision and the Passover. Has the Gospel in its fuller grace nothing for the family? Has the Head of the church repealed that law which for four thousand years brought unspeakable blessings to children? Where is the repeal? Was it by the mouth of Peter, saying the promise is to you and to your children? Did He annul that principle when Paul said to the jailer, believe on the Lord Jesus and thou shalt be saved and thy house?

If that principle was repealed, why is there not only no record of it, but no complaint about it? Jewish converts were very slow to give up ceremonial observances.

But did they give up all the rights of their children without a whisper of complaint? How impossible!

Consider also that there is no such break between the Old and New Church as our brethren suppose. The New Church has the same scriptures—the same promises—is built not only upon apostles, but upon prophets—is grafted into and partakes of the fatness of the good olive tree, Rom. 11. While Jews and proselytes brought their families with them into the kingdom, yet if one parent remained an idolater the children were excluded. Is this the law of the New Testament? Nay. It is more comprehensive than Judaism. 1 Cor. 7 : 14, The children are clean, and so suitable to be offered to God when but one parent is a believer.

In the days of the prophets, God said, "Thou hast taken thy sons and thy daughters whom thou hast borne unto me, and these hast thou sacrificed; . . . thou hast slain my children." Ez. 16: 20, 21. Are not children born unto God now as well as then?

Was it wrong then to turn them over to idols and yet not wrong now to deny that they belong to God?

Consider also that all the historic churches, Greek, Roman, Armenian, Coptic, baptize their children. Some retain also circumcision. How came infant baptism into them all, unless from the teaching of Apostles. Origen says they received it from the Apostles? The Council of Carthage was asked to decide if baptism, like circumcision, must be on the eighth day. Did the Church understand that infants' rights had been abolished? They decided that baptism need not be on the eighth day, but at an early period. When Pelagius was teaching that infants had no original sin, and was accused then of denying baptism to them, he said, not only he did not, but that he had not heard of the most impious heretic that denied infant baptism. Pelagius was born in England, traveled over Europe, Africa and Palestine. If there had been a sect in Christendom refusing to baptize children, he would have found it. But our brethren try to neutralize this historical argument. They find a Tertullian who advises a *delay* of baptism in the case of children and young people, that baptism might wash away as many sins as possible.

The error then was rife that water co-acted with the Spirit in cleansing the soul. Tertullian advised delay, to have the greatest benefit in sweeping away accumulated sins. But the very advice to delay proves the existence of the rite. If there was no such practice, would a sane man ask that it be postponed? And when his reason for it was a mere superstition that baptism effaced guilt, how absurd to make such advice weigh more against baptism than the writings of all the Fathers for it.

Consider the practice of the Apostle of the Gentiles. When Lydia's heart was opened to the gospel, she was baptized and her family. There is no record of any faith but hers. After baptism, she grounded her plea not upon the family's faith, but she said, If ye have judged *me* to be faithful (Gr., pistane, believing), abide in my house. Most Baptist writers cite the jailer's family as believing; but any Greek scholar will tell them that Acts 16 : 34 ascribes faith to the jailer *only.* Believing in God, he rejoiced with all his house, is the literal rendering. The Apostle had promised, " believe on the Lord Jesus, and thou shalt be saved and thy *family."* Acts 16 : 34 records that he did *believe.* And when any Greek scholar says that this text ascribes faith to the family also, you may know he misrepresents the record. Believing is a participle nominative singular, agreeing with jailer.

1 Cor. 1 : 16 teaches that Paul baptized the family of Stephanas; but did not remember baptizing any other family, because Christ sent him not so much to baptize as to evangelize. Stephanas was a disciple present with Paul when he wrote to the Corinthians. It is certain from 1 Cor. 16 : 15 he was a believer. Paul baptized not Stephanas, but his family. And when he adds, after oikon of Stephanas, tina allon, it shows how customary

was family baptism. He baptized his family, but did not recall any other family. He thanked God that he baptized only Crispus and Gaius, lest people should say he had baptized them into his own name. Did this imply that baptism was withdrawn from adults? He baptized two adults and one family, and did not remember a second at Corinth. If adult baptism is continued, how certain, then, is family baptism. As in the Old, so in the New Covenant, parents took their families.

See, Paul salutes families, commends Noah's faith in building an ark to save his family. Peter says the like figure saves us. But how it grates upon that likeness to say the family is excluded!

See Peter's work first opening the Church to the Gentiles. The angel promised Cornelius, Peter shall speak words to thee by which thou shalt be saved and thy family. Acts 11: 14. And Peter seeing the Spirit fall upon Cornelius and family and friends, arranged that they should be baptized. Acts 10: 44, 48.

Did Peter do wrong in baptizing the family with Cornelius and kinsmen? Did the angel misunderstand the constitution of the Church? Did he promise too much, saying Peter shall tell thee words by which thy family shall be saved? How evident is it that neither the apostles nor angels yet knew that children were turned out of the Church of God!

Matt. 18: 5 commends receiving little children as receiving Christ. Are they then unfit to receive the outward sign that they belong to him? Was there ever a shepherd who thought it a profanation to put his mark upon his lambs? Has Jesus recalled the command, " feed my lambs?"

Gal. 3 teaches that the blessing of Abraham has come on the Gentiles, that to Abraham and his seed were the promises made, that if we be Christ's, we are Abraham's seed and heirs according to the promise—that the law four hundred and thirty years after the covenant cannot disannul it. Does this change, then, the foundation-principle of the Church? Has the Gospel taken away what the law could not do? Paul taught the opposite. In all God's covenants parents acted for their offspring. Parents could lay up iniquity for their children. Job 21 : 19. Children from the days of Abel to Zacharias could suffer for the parents' sins, lie in exile for them, and confess them. Dan. 9. But is there nothing in contrast with this evil?—"His blood be on us and on our children," was the imprecation. Israel is still suffering for it. Can the curse run through a thousand generations, while "the promise" ends with parents? Nay, nay, nay. This principle underlies all governments. It is in the very organization of society. It was on this principle that John was circumcised. Lev. 1 : 59, and the infant Jesus was taken to the temple and presented to the Lord. Luke 2 : 22. How impossible, then, for this principle to be inoperative now!

Again and again we are assured the seed of the righteous is blessed; that God loves children for their parents' sake; that He claims that. as the souls of parents, so the souls of

children are His. Ez. 18 : 4. The objection
that the babe is unconscious, has no more
weight against infant baptism than it has
against circumcision, than it had against
Christ's blessing infants, than it had against
presenting the infant Saviour to the Lord.
If the sign of devotion was good from Abraham to John the Baptist, is it not as good
to Gentiles, who, as stones, have been raise
up as spiritual children unto Abraham? If
Abraham's faith brought blessings to his race
—if David's secured favors for his seed—if
parents' faith in Egypt saved the first born—
if the Syrophenician's brought health to her
daughter—if Jairus' brought life to his dead
child, and if the centurion's faith brought
healing to his slave, cannot faith now bring
anything to children? Are such narratives
misleading and delusive? Do they not confirm the command, " disciple," baptizing and
teaching all nations? Yea, when our Lord
has assembled His people at the last, He will
apply this principle, saying to the Father,
" behold, I and the children which God
hath given me." Heb. 2 : 13.

Our brethren object, there is no command. Answer:—1. There is no command to be called Baptist, none to publish a Baptist Bible, none to immerse. There is no command to pray in families, none to observe the first day of the week, none for women to commune. But all God's covenant dealings imply this filial relation, all governments recognize it, all the Apostles taught it, and all their churches practice it to this day.

2. Let children first believe. Answer:— The brepha infants were not required first to believe; the first born in Egypt had not first to believe; the infant Jesus had not first to believe before circumcision; the infant Jew now in exile has not first to believe before it suffers; the Syrophenician's daughter had not first to believe, nor had Jairus' dead child first to believe. Has not a parent's faith as much power now? Can Dr. Anderson and Prof. Curtis write of the Jailer's family "it is explicitly affirmed that they were all believers?" Had those brethren read their Greek Testament they would find

believing agreeing with Jailer only. So the Jailer and Lydia and Cornelius and Stephanas by faith, like Noah, saved their families. Were these families without children?

CHAPTER XII.

HISTORICAL EVIDENCE.

THE history of the Apostles in the Acts extends to 63 A.D. One has counted forty-eight names of converts in the New Testament. The baptism of seven of them is recorded, and with them four families. If this ratio four to seven is applied to the forty-eight, it gives twenty-seven families baptized. But the ratio may have been even more. Not only did the four Crispus, Lydia, Cornelius and the Jailer, accept infant baptism, but the Eunuch is reported to have returned home, established a Christian Church, which to this day baptizes infants. Some followers of Simon Magus also baptized their children. Saul, another of the seven, we find baptized children. So the proportion of four to seven may be six to seven.

But with four to seven for the ratio, in one hundred thousand converts there would have been fifty-seven thousand families. Here is one of the sources of the rapid growth of the early church. Parents took their children with them into the kingdom, and trained them for Christ. May not loose notions about children's obligations now hinder the growth of the Church? Are not multitudes justifying their neglect of worship by this evil theory that parent's faith and example cannot obligate children?

President Dwight has collected the following testimony from the Fathers. Was he able to weigh such evidence?

1. Justin Martyr writes of persons made disciples of Christ from their infancy. That infancy was from the year 70 A.D., so in the days of the Apostles.

2. Irenæus was a disciple of Polycarp, John's convert. He writes of the great pleasure he had in hearing Polycarp repeat the teachings of our Lord as John taught him. He writes, Christ came "to save

infants and little ones and children and youths and elder persons who are born again." By born again, President Dwight says Irenæus " means baptized as he elsewhere shows." Here was a witness only a few years after John.

3. Origen, born 184. The Church hath received the tradition from the Apostles that baptism ought to be administered to infants.

4. Cyprian writes of the decision of sixty-six ministers in council at Carthage, " that no infant is to be prohibited from the benefit of baptism, although but just born." The question asked of the Council was, ought baptism be on the eighth day?

5. Gregory Nazianzen exhorts parents to offer their children to God in baptism.

6. Augustine, of the fourth century— "The whole Church practices infant baptism. It was not instituted by Councils, but was always in use." "Had not read of one Catholic or heretic who maintained that baptism ought to be denied to infants." "This the Church has always maintained."

7. Pelagius—"Who can be so impious as to hinder the baptism of infants?"

Here are seven of the leading writers of the Church from the Apostles down to the fourth century. What folly to deny all this evidence because Tertullian asked that baptism be delayed in the case of children and youths and unmarried people!

One who has studied history a great deal finds:

1. For four hundred years Tertullian was the only one asking delay.

2. For the next seven hundred years none asked for or even delayed baptism.

3. In 1120 a sect arose denying infant salvation and so, by inference, ruled out infant baptism—a sect soon immersed into nothingness.

4. In 1522, five years after the Glorious Reformation, the Anabaptists revived the error.

And, moreover, on the graves of children are engraved all the peculiar appellations of Christians. They are called by the very names the Holy Spirit gives to Christians. They are called holy, believing; said to repose in the bosom of Abraham, Isaac and Jacob; repose in peace among the saints—in the peace of the Lord Jesus. If Paul distinguished Christians by such terms as holy, believing, faithful saints, what did Paul's converts mean when they wrote these words on the graves of their little ones? The catacombs of Rome testify to the infant membership of the early churches. Thousands of children, as well as parents, also died there for Jesus. Their friends recorded their devotion. An acquaintance visited the catacombs. He confirms all that has been given in such testimony. The very stones of the tombs cry out against depriving children of their place in the church of God.

CHAPTER XIII.

THE RELATION OF BAPTIZED CHILDREN TO THE CHURCH.

THERE is no difficulty in understanding that children are in the State, with rights and duties. Why cannot children be "of the kingdom" in the same way? They are under the care of the Church, are to be trained up for Christ. As soon as they have the qualifications as in the State so in the Church they are to perform the duty of members. In the Protestant Church these qualifications are knowledge and piety. See Confess. of Faith, page 436, and Meth. Discipline, page 30. The Churches so practicing get as good members in the judgment of the world as those who deny infant baptism.

How wrong is the charge "that piety is not required," "that these Churches receive members without conversion."

CHAPTER XIV.

CONCLUSION.

1. It is in accord with apostolic practice to transfer Baptizo, not to translate it.

2. There is no duty, then, resting upon the Church to expend millions to introduce immerse or dip. These words do not respond to Baptizo in its varied meanings. The effort to make them has signally failed even with Baptists. They disuse their own Bible, after millions expended for it.

3. Baptism for party divisions is misused. Unity is the Bible idea of "the one baptism." A baptism to be the badge of division, is contrary to the essence of Scriptural baptism, which is "all into one body."

4. When the Pharisees made a handle of Jesus baptizing more disciples than John,

91

Jesus retired from Judea into Galilee. This is opposite to the spirit which crowds upon the work of others, seeking proselytes to our mode of administration, to our church, as more pure for its immersion.

5. If the authority of dictionaries is allowed its force, if the one baptism by the Spirit is the model, if the example of Apostles is followed, baptism must be *with*, not *into*, water, and families as well as individuals must receive baptism.

6. The Church erred by adding exorcism, oil, white robes, processions and nude washings to the simple ordinance.

7. There is no consistent agreement among Baptist writers differing about Baptizo and the prepositions used with it. Truth is consistent. Error originates disagreement.

8. God's people, — called elect, chosen, beloved, family,—always embraced children with covenant privileges. When the New Testament calls His people by their new name (Isa. 62 : 2)—Christians—the Church yet does not lose its identity. When the

natural branches are broken off and the kingdom taken from unbelieving Jews, then the Gentiles are made the inheritors of the promises made to Israel. This truth, so often asserted, secures the rights of children.

9. The Westminster Assembly of 1644, after hearing the Baptist members two or three days plead for immersion as one mode of baptism wisely rejected it.